The Girls' Guide to

WEREWOLVES

Everything Charming about
These Shape-Shifters

Jen Jones

www.raintreepublishers.co.uk
Visit our website to find out
more information about
Raintree books.

To order:

☎ Phone 0845 6044371
🖹 Fax +44 (0) 1865 312263
📧 Email myorders@raintreepublishers.co.uk

Customers from outside the UK please telephone +44 1865 312262

Raintree is an imprint of Capstone Global
Library Limited, a company incorporated in
England and Wales having its registered office
at 7 Pilgrim Street, London, EC4V 6LB
– Registered company number: 6695582

First published by Capstone Press, a
Capstone imprint in 2011
First published in the United Kingdom in
paperback in 2012
The moral rights of the proprietor have
been asserted.

Edited by Kathryn Clay and Laura Knowles
Designed by Tracy Davies
Media research by Marcie Spence
Originated by Capstone Global Library Ltd
Printed and bound in China by South China
Printing Company Ltd

ISBN 978 1 406 24242 3 (paperback)
16 15 14 13 12
10 9 8 7 6 5 4 3 2 1

**British Library Cataloguing in
Publication Data**
Jones, Jen.
Werewolves. -- (Girls' guide to everything
unexplained)
398.4'69-dc23
A full catalogue record for this book is
available from the British Library.

Acknowledgements
We would like to thank the following for
permission to reproduce photographs: Alamy
Images: Mary Evans Picture Library, 13,
Redmond Durrell, 5; AP Images: 15; Capstone
Press: 9 (all), 17 (all); iStockphoto: Curt_
Pickens, 25 (middle), logoff, 4, mrohner, 19
(top), Renphoto, 6, twildlife, 18, VikaValter,
19 (bottom); Kobal Collection, The: Wolfkill,
28 (bottom); Newscom: a11/Zuma Press,
29 (middle), Famous-Ace Pictures, 28 (top),
Summit Entertainment/Temple Hill Ent./
Maverick Films/Imprint/French, Kimberly, 7, 21
(bottom), Universal Pictures, 26, World History
Archive, 27 (bottom); Shutterstock: Alhovik,
cover (scratches), Allyson Kitts, cover (house),
balaikin, 19 (middle), Galushko Sergey, 27
(top), JB Manning, 27 (middle), Kane513, 25
(bottom), Kynata, cover (girl silhouette), Myotis,
21 (top), Photosani, cover (wolf), 25 (top), S.M.,
11; Supplied by Capital Pictures, 29 (bottom);
Wikimedia: 29 (top).

Every effort has been made to contact copyright
holders of any material reproduced in this book.
Any omissions will be rectified in subsequent
printings if notice is given to the publisher.

Disclaimer
All the internet addresses (URLs) given in this
book were valid at the time of going to press.
However, due to the dynamic nature of the
internet, some addresses may have changed, or
sites may have changed or ceased to exist since
publication. While the author and publisher
regret any inconvenience this may cause readers,
no responsibility for any such changes can be

Contents

Some words are shown in **bold**, like this. You can find out what they mean by looking in the word bar at the bottom of the page, or in the glossary.

Chapter 1

Full moon fever

Imagine being able to turn into a bird, snake, or other animal, any time you like. Welcome to the world of **shape-shifters**. Perhaps the most famous form of shape-shifter is a powerful beast that is half man and half wolf. These creatures howl, hunt, and travel in packs.

Werewolves run wild at night.

During the day, werewolves look just like everyone else. Yet by night, they become hairy, hungry creatures on the hunt.

Werewolves can be born or made. They can transform at will or during a full moon. Some people become werewolves after being bitten or scratched by another werewolf. Other people are born werewolves. Still others are cursed. In the Demonata book series, the Grady family has a curse in their bloodline. Grady children turn into werewolves in their teenage years.

How can you tell if you're facing a werewolf? Waiting for the moon to come out isn't going to help. While some people turn into werewolves during a full moon, others transform while under stress. Some can transform whenever they want!

Is that a wolf or a werewolf you hear?

FACT

One of the oldest known ways to become a werewolf is to drink water from the paw print left by a wolf.

shape-shifter: one that can change form or identity at will

How does one become a werewolf? Legends have varied over time. Years ago, people believed it was as easy as putting on a belt made of wolf skin. Still others say it can happen if a person is bitten or scratched by a werewolf.

For years, werewolves were often shown as scary and evil.

Sharp teeth are only one fearsome werewolf feature.

Recent books and films have changed the way we look at werewolves. Clever characters like Jacob Black in the Twilight series and Remus Lupin in the Harry Potter series have made werewolves into celebrities. Now they're heartthrobs and heroes! Whatever their nature, there is no doubt that werewolves are among the smartest, fiercest beasts in the bunch.

Thanks to their impressive makeover process, werewolves have been featured in movies, books, fairy tales, and TV series. Turn the page to see werewolves who have become stars.

Taylor Lautner as Jacob Black

FOLLOW the FANTASY
Page-Turning Reads

Much of our understanding of werewolves comes from stories on the printed page. Werewolves are sometimes hairy and scary but never boring. It makes sense that these creatures are often featured in a good story. If you love things that howl and growl in the night, don't miss these page-turners.

Blood and Chocolate by Annette Curtis Klause

Can a werewolf have a normal life? Sixteen-year-old Vivian hopes so. After the death of her father, the pack leader, Vivian's life is filled with problems. A rival gang threatens to expose the pack's secret. An **alpha** werewolf wants to make Vivian his mate. And Vivian falls in love with a human. Will Vivian choose her pack or expose her secret for love?

alpha: high-ranking member of a group of animals

The Witchy Worries of Abbie Adams by Rhonda Hayter

It's not always easy being 11 years old, especially if you're Abbie Adams. Sure, she's dealing with regular stuff such as homework, mean teachers, and practising for the school play. But most people don't know that she's a witch and her younger brother is a werewolf. From time travel to hairy brothers, there's never a dull moment in this book!

Red Rider's Hood by Neal Shusterman

The classic fairy tale is all grown up in this twist on *Little Red Riding Hood*. Meet Red Rider. He's a boy with a hot red Mustang car and a werewolf-hunting grandma. Lurking within Grandma's neighbourhood is a dangerous gang known as the Wolves. To learn the Wolves' secrets, Red Rider goes undercover and joins the pack. Things get complicated when he learns they are werewolves.

Chapter 2

Howlin' history

Maybe you think that werewolves are purely make-believe. But plenty of people suspect that werewolves are all too real. In 1988 nearly 350,000 people called a hotline set up to promote the television show *Werewolf*. Many of the callers reported werewolf sightings.

Some people even claim to be werewolves!

Of course, werewolf sightings are nothing new. For hundreds of years, people all over the world have passed down real-life **lupine** legends. So are werewolves true creatures of the night, or do they simply make a good story?

Do werewolves go "bump" in the night?

lupine: having wolf-like qualities

THE FIRST WEREWOLF

Werewolf legends began in early Greek **mythology**. It all started with the Greek king Lycaon. To punish Lycaon for his cruel ways, the gods turned him into a wolf. Stories differ on how Lycaon was transformed, but one thing is certain – he is considered the first werewolf. Lycaon's name inspired the word "lycanthropy", which means a magical ability to become a wolf. The Roman writer Ovid's famous poem "Metamorphoses" also tells his story.

Many Europeans believed that werewolves were taken over by the devil.

Many werewolf stories also came from common beliefs during the Middle Ages. Throughout Europe, serial killings and actual wolf attacks led to the spread of werewolf fears.

Werewolf legends have been around for centuries.

In 1589, German farmer Peter Stumpp was put on trial for being a werewolf. Stumpp admitted to killing 16 people, but he said it was the devil's doing. He claimed the devil had given him a belt. The belt turned him into a greedy, devouring wolf with a huge body, sharp teeth, and strong paws.

mythology: collection of myths from a culture

REAL-LIFE WEREWOLVES

Werewolf fever continued into the modern day. In the 1970s, Canadian doctors reported several cases of wolf-like behaviour. The patients shared stories of howling at the moon, discovering strange powers, and sleeping in graveyards.

In 2007, Danny Ramos Gomez was featured on a TV programme. He had earned the nickname "Wolf Man", due to a medical condition. A disease nicknamed the "werewolf **syndrome**" left his body covered with hair. Though a rare condition, people throughout the world have reported carrying the disease.

The werewolf craze appears to be invading schools as well.

syndrome: group of at least three symptoms or signs that occur together and characterize a disease

Recent news reports have shared claims of real-life teen werewolves. In San Antonio, Texas, at least six wolf packs are said to be on the loose. The packs claim to have up to 20 werewolves each. So are they true werewolves or just teens copying their favourite flicks? No one knows for sure. But the growing number of werewolf reports definitely blurs the line between fact and fantasy.

There have been fewer than 200 reports of werewolf syndrome.

FOLLOW the FANTASY ON SCREEN

For years Hollywood has been putting werewolves in the spotlight. Some of the first werewolf flicks were *The Werewolf* (1913), *Werewolf of London* (1935), and *The Wolf Man* (1941). *I Was a Teen Werewolf* (1957) and *Teen Wolf* (1985) still hold their appeal as werewolf films today. Though the special effects have got better over time, the excitement and mystery remains the same. See their appeal for yourself in these modern werewolf films:

The Twilight Saga

Forget Edward Cullen. For werewolf fans, "Team Jacob" is the place to be. The movies are based on the popular book series by Stephenie Meyer. Audiences are introduced to human Bella, vampire Edward, and werewolf Jacob. The trio becomes part of a battle between vampires and werewolves in their small Washington town.

Werewolf of Fever Swamp

Twilight isn't the only book featuring werewolves to be turned into a film. Enter *Werewolf of Fever Swamp*, based on R. L. Stine's Goosebumps series. The film tells the story of Grady, a young boy whose family moves to the swamps of Florida, USA. His new town is full of werewolf mysteries and legends, not to mention a Swamp Hermit.

The Brothers Grimm

This action-packed film follows Wilhelm and Jacob Grimm, played by Matt Damon and Heath Ledger. The brothers get mixed up in a tale of black magic. They face a witch, a werewolf, and other supernatural creatures. The brothers must learn to recognize what is real and what is fantasy in order to break the witch's spell.

Chapter 3

Beauty of
the beast

Much like their on-screen images, werewolves really are larger than life. In fact, legends tell us that they can be up to 2.4 metres (8 feet) tall and have strength to match their size. So what else sets werewolves apart? There are plenty of ways to spot a werewolf, even if you're not running with the pack. Find useful clues in the following ferocious features.

Can you tell the difference between wolves and werewolves?

Glowing eyes: Keep a look out for glowing eyes in the night. Some werewolves have humanlike brown or green eyes. Others have bright gold eyes, like Michael Jackson's character in the music video for "Thriller". When in human form, a werewolf might also have eyebrows that meet in the middle.

Fur coat: Werewolves are covered in fur that comes out in full force when they shape-shift. Even as humans, the fur is always there. It just hides under the skin's surface. Many werewolves also sprout whiskers when they transform.

Sharp teeth: Werewolves usually grow sharp fang-like teeth. All the better to tear into their prey, my dear!

Pointy ears: Like most **canines**, werewolves can hear high-pitched and faraway sounds better than humans can. Perhaps that's why their ears turn pointy when they shape-shift. They're zoning in on their target!

Big claws: Werewolves grow large paws designed for capturing victims. Long, curved claws help them dig into their catch.

canine: dog or dog-like animal

WAKE UP, WOLF

In many cases, people discover their werewolf side during a full moon.

When this werewolf change happens for the first time, it's known as an awakening. Often, this can happen during the teen years. In the Twilight series, every member of the Quileute wolf pack transforms as a teen. Pack leader Sam Uley is the first and the oldest, aged 19. Fifteen-year-old Seth Clearwater is the youngest.

FACT

The Twilight wolves can transform, or "phase", whenever they want.

Are you afraid of a full moon?

The Twilight wolf pack

QUIZ: Is your BFF a she-wolf?

Do you think your BFF could be a werewolf in disguise? Take this quiz and find out — if you dare!

When your BFF wants to relax, she:

a) goes for a run through the woods.

b) gets a manicure. Her nails are always so long!

c) rests by the pool.

d) takes a long afternoon nap in a dark corner.

Your BFF can't stop talking about:

a) Taylor Lautner

b) Tyler Posey

c) Nick Jonas

d) Robert Pattinson

Your BFF decides to get a dog. She adopts a:

a) German Shepherd

b) huskie

c) fluffy Pomeranian

d) bloodhound

Who's your BFF's favourite Twilight character?

a) Jacob Black

b) Leah Clearwater

c) Bella Swan

d) Edward Cullen

 Where would your BFF love to get a part-time job?

a) a dog pound

b) a vet clinic

c) a book shop

d) a blood bank

 What is your BFF's favourite werewolf book?

a) Not sure – she always changes the subject when I bring it up.

b) She loves any story with a werewolf in it.

c) She'll read a werewolf book but doesn't have any favourites.

d) Books about werewolves? She hates them!

Look through your answers to see if your BFF is leader of the wolf pack. If you circled:

Mostly As: Your BFF definitely plays for Team Jacob.

Mostly Bs: You may want to avoid moonlight strolls with your BFF. It's possible she's a werewolf.

Mostly Cs: No need to worry. Your BFF is human as can be.

Mostly Ds: She's not a werewolf, but you'll want to keep some garlic nearby. It sounds like she might be a vampire!

Chapter 4

Who's afraid of the big bad wolf?

Killing animals, and sometimes people, is all part of a werewolf's animal **instinct**. But because they are part human, werewolves are expected to follow human laws. As such, they often get the criminal treatment. In France during the 1500s, thousands of suspected werewolves were put on trial for attacking villagers.

Yet werewolves can also use their amazing powers for protecting others. Anyone who's read the Twilight books knows that they have a soft side. Whether used for good or evil, there is no doubt that werewolves have some serious strengths.

instinct: behaviour that is natural rather than learned

Shape-shifting: Perhaps the coolest thing that werewolves do is shape-shift from human form into wolf form. For many werewolves, it happens automatically during a full moon. Others can do it on command. The idea of shape-shifting started with American Indians. Many of their legends describe humans turning into animals. These people are called skin-walkers.

The need for speed: Werewolves run with unbelievable speed on all fours like wolves. In the Twilight series, Jacob and his fellow werewolves race through the forest in search of vampires. Though vampires are also known for their speed, there is usually no outrunning a werewolf.

Strong senses: Imagine being able to see, smell, or hear like a superhero. Werewolves can do just that. From seeing in the dark to hearing things from far away, werewolves' senses are super sharp.

Werewolf weaknesses

Catching a werewolf is no easy task. But killing one is even harder. What is powerful enough to take down a werewolf? Like zombies, the most successful way to kill a werewolf is to cut off its head! Yet there are other ways to stop a werewolf in its tracks. Keep reading to find out what makes werewolves weak.

Would you know how to fend off a werewolf?

Full moon: For shape-shifters, a full moon can certainly be an unwelcome sight. Imagine if you were hanging out with friends or had an important event and forgot what day it was. Full moons are known for causing strange happenings, and werewolf transformations are no exception. The first film to show a werewolf changing under a full moon was 1941's *The Wolf Man*.

Silver: Regular weapons won't harm a werewolf. Silver bullets and knives are the only weapons that can kill or cause injury to a werewolf. For many werewolves, their skin will burn if they even touch silver. In the US comedy flick *My Mom's a Werewolf*, Harry is a werewolf who refuses to use silverware when eating. He meets his end when stabbed by a silver knife.

Monkshood: An ingredient often used in witches' brew, monkshood is said to have first come from the drool of Hercules' evil three-headed dog. Some say anyone who eats monkshood will turn into a werewolf. The more common belief is that monkshood is actually poisonous to werewolves. The jury is still out on this toxic plant's powers, but one thing is for sure – it is very poisonous to humans.

Sticky scars: When werewolves get hurt, their scars can often be seen even when they are in human form. Telltale scars make them easier to spot.

✣ ✣ ✣ ✣ ✣ ✣ ✣ ✣ ✣ ✣ ✣ ✣ ✣ ✣ ✣ ✣ ✣

WEREWOLVES' AWARDS

Biggest Heartthrob
Jacob Black (Twilight series)

This werewolf doesn't win Bella's heart, but he's definitely not lacking in fans. They're all Team Jacob!

Most Valuable Player
Scott Howard (Teen Wolf)

Follow Scott's transformation from scrawny reserve basketball player to king of slam dunks.

Most Likely Hero
Link (*The Legend of Zelda: Twilight Princess*)

This part wolf/part human is all hero. You control Link as he saves his homeland from the evil Twilight Realm in this wolf-packed computer game.

Perfect Theme Song
***She-Wolf* by Shakira**

This chart-topping hit tells the story of living life as a human in disguise.

Best Wizarding Werewolf
Remus Lupin (The Harry Potter series)

Though a werewolf, Remus was able to teach Harry Potter the powerful Patronus spell.

GLOSSARY

alpha high-ranking member of a group of animals

canine dog or dog-like animal

instinct behaviour that is natural rather than learned

lupine having wolf-like qualities

mythology collection of myths from a culture

shape~shifter one that can change form or identity at will

syndrome group of at least three symptoms or signs that occur together and characterize a disease

FIND OUT MORE

How to Love a Werewolf, Sophie Collins (Spruce, 2010)

The Mystery of Vampires and Werewolves (Can Science Solve?) Chris Oxlade (Heinemann Library, 2008)

The Undead, Jim Pipe (TickTock Books, 2008)

Werewolf Attack! (Clash), John Townsend, (Crabtree, 2008)

The Werewolf Hunter's Guide (Monster Tracker), Ursula Lestrade (Franklin Watts, 2012)

Werewolves (Monster Mania), John Malam (QED, 2011)

Werewolves (Mythical Creatures), Rebecca Rissman (Raintree, 2010)

INDEX